HOT DIGGITY DOG

THE History OF THE HOT DOG

Adrienne Sylver

ILLUSTRATED BY
Elwood H. Smith

PUFFIN BOOKS

PUFFIN BOOKS
An imprint of Penguin Random House LLC
375 Hudson Street
New York, New York 10014

First published in the United States of America by Dutton Children's Books,
a division of Penguin Young Readers Group, 2010
Published by Puffin Books, an imprint of Penguin Random House LLC, 2015

Text copyright © 2010 by Adrienne Sylver
Illustrations copyright © 2010 by Elwood H. Smith

Photo of hot dog and bun used on jacket and pp. 26-27, photo of cooked hot dog on p. 21,
photo of fruit in cups and ice cream in cup on p. 28 courtesy of iStock;
photo of earth (globe) used on p. 5 courtesy of StockXchng;
Library of Congress is the source for the public domain background photo of the New York City panorama on pp. 10-11.

LIBRARY OF CONGRESS CATALOGING-IN-PUBLICATION DATA IS AVAILABLE.

Puffin Books ISBN 978-0-14-751578-0

Manufactured in China
Designed by Irene Vandervoort

1 3 5 7 9 10 8 6 4 2

For my family,
Mike, Nick, and Meaghan.
I love you more than
all the hot dogs in the world!

—AS

In loving memory of my sister,
Jude, who loved to dip her hot dogs
(straight up, no bun) in a pool
of ketchup.

—ES

It's the Fourth of July. Red, white, and blue streamers decorate the park. Fireworks will boom in the sky tonight. And what will Americans be eating? Hot dogs!

Hot dogs are one of America's favorite foods, especially during the summer. In fact, if you line up the two billion hot dogs we eat each July, they would stretch more than 190,000 miles. That's enough to circle the Earth seven times!

How did hot dogs become such a popular treat? The answer to that mystery is a fun journey through history and a peek into cultures around the world. The story begins thousands of years ago in Europe.

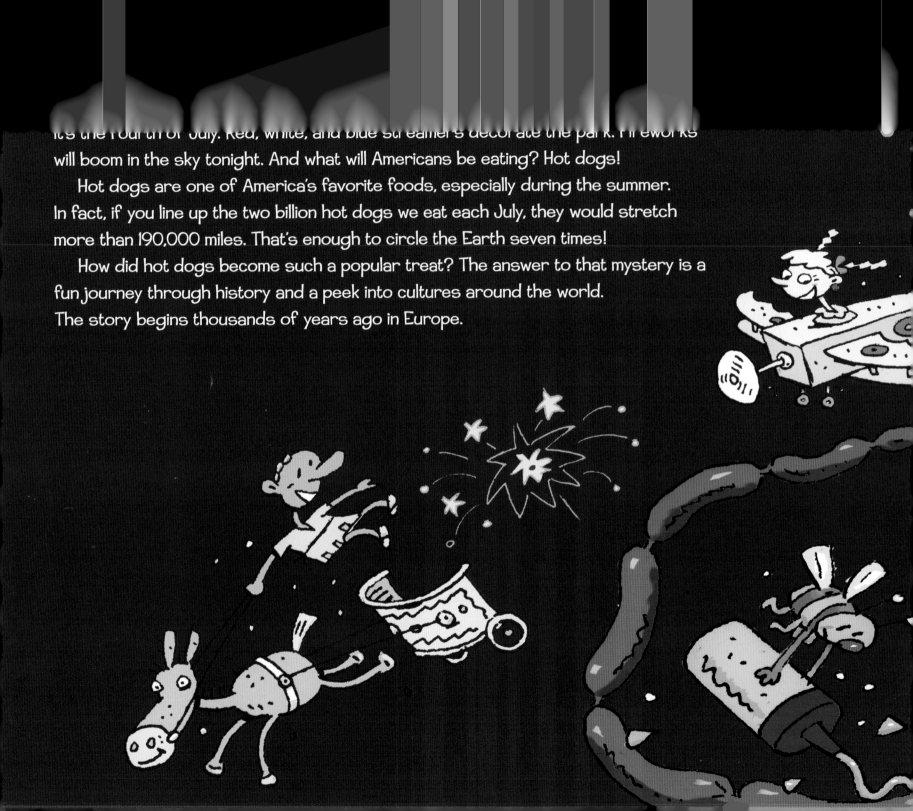

"Franks," "Wieners," and "Red Hots"

are nicknames for hot dogs.

Keep reading to find out how
the hot dog earned its funny names.

A Hot Date

More franks are eaten in July
than in any other month.
Maybe that's why July is National Hot Dog Month.
It's also National Ice Cream, Watermelon,
Baked Beans, and Blueberry Month!

In the Beginning

Hot dogs are a kind of sausage. So, where does sausage come from?

It's one of history's oldest meals. In fact, sausage is old enough to be mentioned in the **ODYSSEY**, an ancient Greek poem.

Sausage became a popular snack with the help of a Roman cook named Gaius. Gaius was a chef for Nero Claudius Caesar, a leader of the mighty Roman Empire. One day, Chef Gaius cut into a roasted pig and noticed its puffy intestines. He decided to make a new dish by stuffing the intestines with spices and ground meat. The Romans loved Gaius's sausage.

Soon Roman festivals featured sausages as delicacies. Word of the tasty treat spread throughout the huge empire.

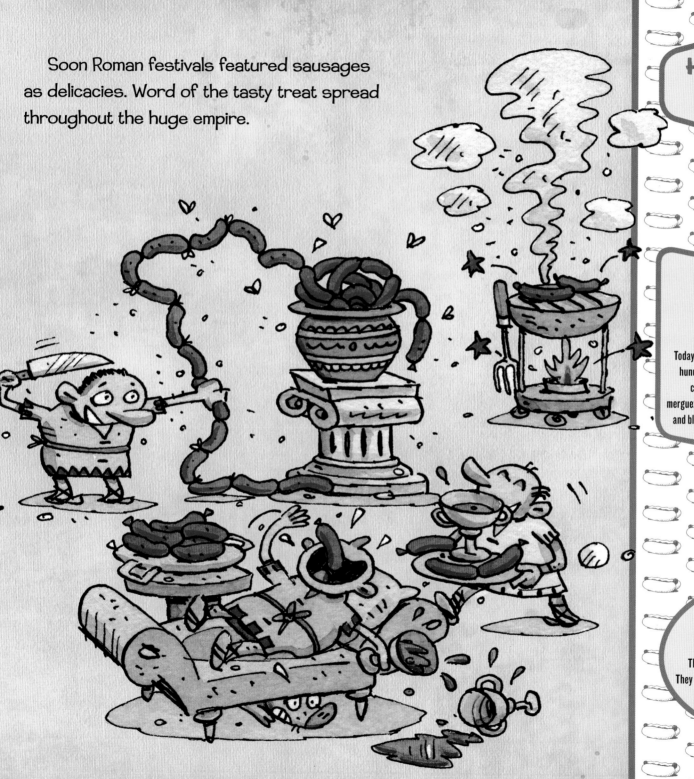

Name Your Dog

Frankfurter and wiener are nicknames for the hot dog—frankfurter from Frankfurt, Germany, and wiener, from the German word **wein**, meaning "Vienna."

What's in a Name?

Who named the hot dog? No one knows for sure. Here's one theory: The shape of a hot dog resembles the shape of a long, skinny dachshund dog. German sausage vendors used to shout, "Get your red hot dachshund sausages!" Over time, the name was shortened.

Happy Birthday, Doggie!

Frankfurt had a huge party in 1987 to celebrate the 500th anniversary of the hot dog in that city.

Mein Name ist Hot Dog

One day, long after the fall of the Roman Empire, a sausage maker invented the recipe for the modern hot dog. But the tasty dog's exact birthplace is an unsolved puzzle. Germans say the first hot dog was made in Frankfurt, Germany, in the 1400s. Austrians claim the first wiener was eaten in Vienna, Austria.

   Wherever the hot dog got its start, there's no mystery about its arrival in the New World. Immigrants from Europe brought the special sausage to America in the 1860s.

Welcome to the U.S.A.

In the nineteenth century, boats crowded with immigrants arrived in America. The new Americans worked long, hard hours. They looked for cheap food that could be prepared quickly. Hot dogs made by German and Austrian immigrants were just the thing for a fast meal. Pushcarts filled with hot dogs began appearing on street corners in big cities.

At first, hot dogs were sold without a bun. Imagine picking your lunch up off the grill with bare fingers. **OUCH!** One vendor gave his customers gloves, but so many people walked off with the expensive mitts that the hot dog seller feared he would go broke. Finally, he asked his brother-in-law, a baker, for help. The baker made a special roll to fit America's favorite sausage. Voilà! The modern hot dog—served in a bun—was born.

Where'd You Get that Donut?

Pilgrims brought the donut to America from Holland. Many of America's favorite foods came from faraway places:

Pizza from Naples, Italy; Ice Cream from China; French Fries from Belgium and France.

May I Have Some Peanut Butter?

Some of the world's favorite foods originally came from North and South America, or the "New World" to European explorers. Peanut butter can be traced back to the Inca Indians in South America. Other foods native to the Americas include potatoes, tomatoes, corn, squash, sunflower seeds, maple sugar, chocolate, and blueberries.

TOP DOGS
Who Eats the Most Hot Dogs?

1. Los Angeles
2. New York
3. Chicago
4. San Antonio
5. Philadelphia

Riding the Hot Dog to Fame

In 1916, Nathan Handwerker opened
a nickel hot dog stand in Coney Island, New York City.
Now, Nathan's Famous hot dogs
can be found all over America.
In 2000, Nathan's Famous was named
the official hot dog of the New York Yankees.

Dogs Fit for a King

In 1939, King George VI of England visited America.
President Franklin D. Roosevelt wanted to serve the king
something special—and especially American.
At a presidential picnic, King George enjoyed a
"delightful hot-dog sandwich."

A Star Is Born

In New York City, the first Coney Island hot dog stand opened in the 1870s.
Back then, you could buy a dog for just five cents! During the Great Depression,
in the 1930s, many people couldn't find jobs that would pay to feed and clothe their
families. Most, however, could afford a nickel for a hot dog.

The cheap, tasty hot dog became more popular than ever.

Take Me Out to the Ball Game

In the late 1800s, hot dog vendors realized that their sausages were easy to cook, eat, and sell almost anywhere—even in crowded baseball stadiums. American sports fans soon came to love hot dogs. It's traditional to chow down on a dog when cheering on your team at a baseball game.

Other countries have their own traditional stadium foods. In Japan, you might snack on edamame, or chilled soybean pods, while watching the ball game. In South Africa, soccer fans eat idombolo (dumplings) or beetroot salad at the match. At Mexican ball parks, fans fill up on empanadas, tamales, and tacos.

EDAMAME

Sports Nutrition?

Baseball great Babe Ruth, who played in the major leagues from 1914–1935, loved hot dogs so much that he'd often eat more than a dozen in one sitting.

Fair Is Foul

In sixteenth-century England, at Shakespeare's Globe Theatre, vendors sold hazelnuts, apples, and oranges. Audiences threw the snacks at actors they didn't like—head's up!

"Fair is foul, and foul fair."—**Macbeth**

Words of Wisdom

"A hot dog at the ball park is better than a steak at the Ritz."
—Humphrey Bogart

HOT DOGS

A Red Hot Takeover

In the mid-1950s, many American women went to work in offices. Few families had time to cook fancy dinners every night. The hot dog was an easy answer for a fast meal. To keep up with demand, hot dog makers opened factories where they could crank out thousands of links at a time.

In 1957, July was declared National Hot Dog Month.

NAME YOUR DOG:

Some Famous Hot Dog Stands

1. Der Wienerschnitzel—Las Vegas, NV

2. Tail O' the Pup—Los Angeles, CA

3. **HILLBILLY HOT DOGS**—Lesage, WV

4. Spike's Junkyard Dogs—Providence, RI

5. Mustard's Last Stand—Evanston, IL

6. Swanky Franks—Norwalk, CT

7. Poochie's—Skokie, IL

8. Wiener World—Pittsburgh, PA

9. Woofie's—Overland, MO

10. **DEMON DOGS**—Chicago, IL

Extreme Advertising

The Oscar Mayer Wienermobile first hit the streets of Chicago in 1936. Today's model sports a removable bun roof, a mustard-splattered walkway, and GPS satellite technology. If you got lost driving a Wienermobile, you could ask your hot dog for directions!

The Hot Dog Farm

How are all these hot dogs made?

   Hot dogs are usually made from a variety of meats, such as beef, pork, chicken, or turkey. Recently, vegetarian "veggie dogs" hit the scene. Each hot dog maker has a secret recipe of meats or vegetables and spices. The meats or veggies are chopped into small parts and blended with bread crumbs, flour, and seasonings. The gooey hot dog batter is pumped into a thin plastic tube to hold it together. Then it's cooked or smoked. Finally, the hot dog takes a bath in cool water, and the plastic is peeled away. The hot dogs are shipped off to supermarkets in refrigerated trucks.

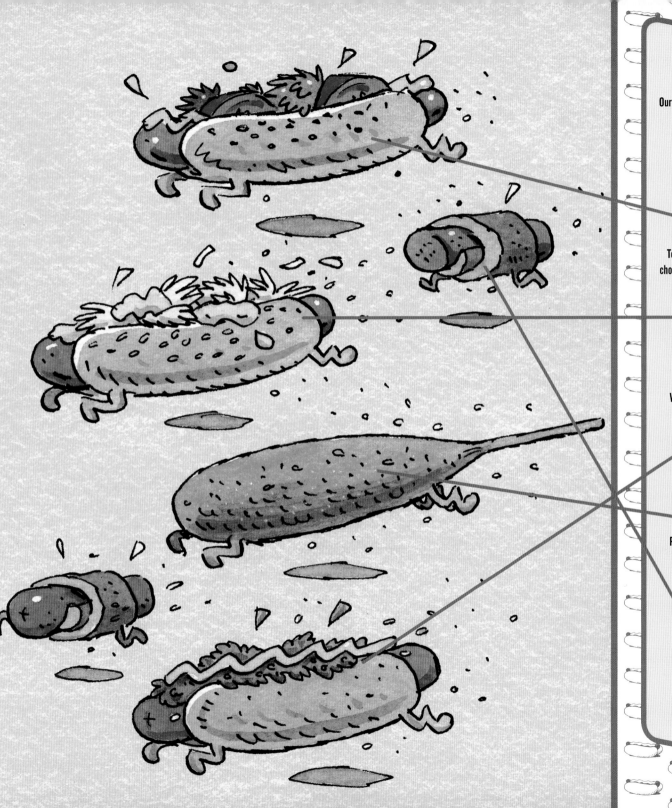

Strange Dogs

Salmon dogs topped with avocados and carrots
are popular at Franktitude, in Miami, Florida.
At Hillbilly Hot Dogs in Lesage, West Virginia,
hot dogs topped with ketchup, cheese, and
scrambled eggs are a big hit.
Movie stars stop in for lunch at Pink's
in Los Angeles, California,
to get the bacon burrito dog.

Mighty Mustard

The ancient Romans ground mustard seeds
and mixed them with water or wine
to make a paste. They used the paste
as a sauce for food and also
to treat war wounds! The mustard plant
was once used to heal everything from toothaches
and snakebites to arthritis.

Pope John XXII, a fourteenth-century pope
from France, was so fond of mustard that he created a
new position—**grand moutardier du pape**
(official mustard-maker for the pope).

Ketchup: A History

In the seventeenth century, European explorers enjoyed
a salty fish sauce called "ketsiap" when they visited China.
British cooks copied it with a sauce called "catsup,"
often made with mushrooms.
When early American settlers discovered tomatoes,
a food native to America, they began
making ketchup with tomatoes.

Grab a Dog

You've grilled it, boiled it, or fried it. Is your stomach growling? You're almost ready to eat. First you have to decide if you want any condiments, or toppings, on your dog. Traditional toppings include mustard, ketchup, chili, chopped sweet pickles, called relish, and pickled cabbage, called sauerkraut. But there are endless possibilities. You can see the diversity of American cuisine, and the American people, in the many different hot dogs we create.

Extreme Eating

Imagine getting paid to eat. Competitive eaters do. There are eating contests for everything from watermelon to chicken wings to asparagus. A group called Major League Eating runs official contests.

Nathan's Famous Fourth of July International Hot Dog Eating Contest has been held each year since 1916 at Coney Island. The winner is the person who can eat the most hot dogs in ten minutes. In recent years, ESPN has broadcast the event, and tens of thousands of fans turn up to watch.

Top Dog

In 2009, Joey Chestnut of San Jose, California, won the International Hot Dog Eating Contest by eating 68 hot dogs and buns in 10 minutes. For his speed-eating efforts, he won $20,000—that's about $294.11 per hot dog. Wow!

Don't Like Hot Dogs?

Eating records have been set for nearly every type of food. There's the 170 M&M's eaten in 3 minutes with chopsticks, 15.25 pounds of strawberry shortcake gobbled in 8 minutes, 71 tamales in 12 minutes, and 26 grilled cheese sandwiches in 10 minutes.

Puppy Pun

Q: Why did the man put a sweater on his hot dog?

A: Because it was a chili dog!

Calling All Dogs

If you have a craving for a hot dog in a foreign place, try this handy hot dog translator:

U.S.A.—Hot dog, red hot

Spain or Cuba—Perro caliente

Germany—Wurst or Heisser Hund

France—Chien chaud

Finland—Makkarat

Netherlands—Worstjes

Portugal—Cachorro quente

Brain Food

College kids like easy to make, tasty food. **The Yale Record** printed a poem in 1895 about a favorite hot dog stand.

"Echoes from the Lunch Wagon"

Tis dogs' delight to bark and bite,

Thus does the adage run.

But I delight to bite the dog

When placed inside a bun.

Healthy Dogs

It's not healthy or safe to stuff yourself like a competitive eater. If you try to eat too much, you could choke or make yourself sick. Professional eaters must be at least eighteen years old, and often follow special diets to gradually stretch their stomachs.

Most nutrition experts agree that too much of any food isn't good for you, but treats every so often are just fine. So, if you love hot dogs, it's okay to eat one once in a while. Hot dogs have some protein, a very important nutrient, but can also be high in fat and sodium (salt), unless you're eating the vegetarian kind.

Future Dogs

Food changes over time. Vegetarian hot dogs have become popular as more Americans pay attention to healthy eating. Organic hot dogs are now made for hot dog lovers who are concerned about the effects of chemicals on the environment and in food. What's in the future for the hot dog? Maybe you'll become famous for discovering a new type of dog. How about a healthy celery dog, a hot dog that can be eaten underwater, or one that can be grown like a plant in outer space?

Invent Your Own Dog

When Russell Emel was seven, he demanded peanut butter on everything. His mother asked a local meat company to make a peanut butter–flavored hot dog. They did. The nutty dogs were a big hit!

Space Dogs

The Apollo 11 astronauts were the first to eat hot dogs in space. It was 1969 when Neil Armstrong became the first person to walk on the moon. Along with their dogs the astronauts enjoyed hot coffee, canned peaches, and sugar cookies.

Beyond the Dog

Check out these food museums:
The Jell-O Museum in LeRoy, New York;
the SPAM® Museum in Austin, Minnesota;
the Hershey Museum, in Hershey, Pennsylvania;
and the National Apple Museum
in Biglerville, Pennsylvania.

Chief Treats

The favorite foods of . . .

GEORGE WASHINGTON: ice cream

ABRAHAM LINCOLN: fruit salad

FRANKLIN D. ROOSEVELT: pancakes

JOHN F. KENNEDY: New England clam chowder

What's Your Story?

All foods have a story. Through the history of food, we can learn about faraway lands and people. Sometimes, the foods we eat can even reveal secrets about our own histories. What do your favorite foods have to say about you?

Whether you adore pickles, corn, or pizza, there are plenty of ways to find out more about your favorite snacks. First, start with your family. Do you have special recipes passed down from your ancestors? You can research food by going to the library or a bookstore, or by doing some detective work on the Internet. Take a trip to a food museum. By the time you're through, you may have enough information for your own book. Certainly, you'll have a happy stomach and a good story!

My Family Recipes

HOT AND TANGY DOGS

This snack recipe was one of my mother's favorites. You don't really taste the mustard.
It just gives the hot dogs a bite!

Two packages of hot dogs

6-8 oz. jelly (grape or any flavor)

1/4 cup mustard (more if you like it spicy)

Cut hot dogs into one-inch pieces. Place jelly and mustard into a frying pan.

Stir over low heat until well blended. Add hot dogs. Cover and simmer up to 1 hour.

Use toothpicks to serve.

CLASSIC FRANKS AND BEANS

An historic favorite! (Makes ten servings, doesn't break the bank.)

5 hot dogs

1 15-oz can kidney beans, drained

1 15-oz can black beans, drained

1 15-oz can butter beans, drained (or substitute your favorite canned bean)

3/4 cup barbeque sauce

Mix all ingredients in a medium saucepan. Bring to a boil on medium heat. Reduce heat and simmer 10 minutes, stirring occasionally. Dish up and enjoy.

Interesting websites:

www.majorleagueeating.com

www.nathansfamous.com

www.kraftfoods.com

www.hot-dog.org

More fun books to read:

SCIENCE EXPERIMENTS YOU CAN EAT by Vicki Cobb. HarperTrophy, 1984.

THE SCIENCE CHEF: 100 FUN FOOD EXPERIMENTS AND RECIPES FOR KIDS by Joan D'Amico and
Karen Eich Drummond. Jossey-Bass, 1994.

Bibliography

Hippisley-Coxe, Antony & Araminta. **THE GREAT BOOK OF SAUSAGES**. New York: Overlook Press,
1987.

Kutas, Rytek. **GREAT SAUSAGE RECIPES AND MEAT CURING**. New York: The Sausage Maker, 1984.

Trager, James. **THE FOOD CHRONOLOGY: A FOOD LOVER'S COMPENDIUM OF EVENTS AND
ANECDOTES, FROM PREHISTORY TO THE PRESENT**. New York: Owl Books, 1997.

Major League Eating Sports Franchise, http://www.majorleagueeating.com/ (New York,
New York, 2007)

Nathan's Famous, http://www.nathansfamous.com/ (Westbury, New York, 2000–2007)

National Hot Dog & Sausage Council, http://www.hot-dog.org/ (Washington, D.C., 1998–2007)

Oscar Mayer/Kraft Foods, http://www.kraftfood.com/om/ (Global Headquarters-Northfield,
Illinois, 2007)